Vitamix Blender Cookbook 2021

1001-Day Super-Easy, Super-Healthy Vitamix Blender Recipes

for All-Natural Meals to Weight Loss, Detox, Energy Boosts, and More

Taera Jodha

Table of Contents

Introduction

The Vitamix blender is a powerful blender that can actually heat up liquids, and it is designed to be used to make soup safely with a built-in steam escape and blades that can heat the soup up. The Vitamix blender is amazing, there are so many things you can make easily and quickly. If you haven't used your Vitamix blender to make soup, this recipe book is the perfect place to start, and you will be amazed at how easy it really is to make these simple but very appetizing soups in your blender.

Many people are excited when they first purchase a Vitamix but aren't really sure what to do with it besides make smoothies. While the Vitamix is great for making smoothies, it has the potential to be used for so much more. The popular recipes and preparation techniques in the Vitamix Blender Cookbook 2021 will inspire you to make delicious and easily prepared blender dishes.

This cookbook contains a plethora of recipes that can all be made quickly and easily right in your Vitamix blender. All of our recipes are designed specifically to be compatible with the Vitamix blender, and to help you get the most out of your investment.

Chapter 1: Basics of Vitamix 5200 Blender

What is Vitamix 5200 Blender?

The Vitamix 5200 blender is one of the advanced and most popular heavy-duty blenders available in the market. The Vitamix blender is tall in size and its simple design gives it classic look. The most reliable and powerful Vitamix blender is capable of breakdown anything that you put into its container. You can heat, blend, chop, puree, and grind whatever you want using a Vitamix blender. The blender comes with powerful Swedish-built motor works on 1380 watts and generates 2 horsepower to spin stainless steel blade at more than 37000 rpm to blend anything smoothly.

The Vitamix 5200 blender is loaded with easy to operate toggle switches and having 10-speed variable controllers to crush ice and grind the toughest ingredients easy to get perfect results. Its stainless steel laser-cut blade handles the toughest ingredients and gives you perfect blending results whenever you make your favorite drink in Vitamix blender. Its 64 oz size clear plastic container is made up of BPA-free Tritan co-polyester material. To make a hot soup Vitamix blender works at high speed to create friction heat and brings your cold ingredients into steaming hot soup within 6 minutes. After each use Vitamix blender is easy to clean itself. You just need to add a drop of dish soap and add some warm water to the container it cleans itself within 30 to 60 seconds. The blender having an advanced cooling system in the motor to keep it cools when it is in use. If the blender motor is overheated then it has an auto-shutoff feature to prevent it from burning. The blenders weigh 10.6 pounds and having the dimension 20.5 x 8.75 x 7.25 inches it takes less space on your kitchen countertop.

Parts and Functions

1. Containers

The Vitamix container comes with 64 oz (2-liters) capacity, 20 inches in height, and also having a clear measurement marking on it. The containers are made up of special impact-resistant BPA-free plastic material known as Eastman Tritan co-polyester. These heavy-duty containers are sitting on a square rubber pad to keep it stable and help to reduce the vibrations caused during the blending process. The container has an ergonomic handle that comes with a soft grip that helps to turn the container while pouring. The container has a special 2-part lid with a removable lid plug. You can remove the lid plug during the blending process to add ingredients. You can also use the tamper to push down the ingredients and remove the air gaps without removing the lid of the container during the blending process.

2. Blade System

The blade of the Vitamix blender is made up of hardened stainless steel aircraft-grade material. The laser-cut blades are made to handle the toughest ingredients easily. The blade has 3 inches in diameter and rotates at 37000 RPM speed to crush, blend, and grind your ingredients smoothly. The blades that come with a container are fixed and non-removable. The non-removable blade is easy to clean but if you want to change the blade you need a wrench or you have to buy a separate container. The blender comes with wet blade options if you want to change the wet blade with a dry blade you need to purchase a dry blade separately as an accessory.

3. Motor

The Vitamix blender comes with powerful Swedish-built motor works on 1380w power and generates 2 horsepower. It rotates blender blades at 37000 RPM to crush and blend your ingredients easily. The motor is equipped with an advanced thermal protection system to prevent burnout and overload protection. The motor also has a radial cooling fan to decrease the motor temperature while it is operational.

4. Control System

The Vitamix control system comes with a simple design and classic look. It comes with two switches and a one-speed controller dial. The switches are made up of soft-touch rubber.

- **ON/OFF Switch:** Using this switch you can easily ON your blender by pushing switch UP and easily OFF your blender by pushing switch DOWN.
- **High/Variable Switch:** High is used for the fastest speed and variable is used to operate the blender at different speeds. Always make sure the High/Variable switch is set at Variable position before pushing the ON/OFF switch. Don't start your blender on High settings.

- **Variable speed controller switch:** This controller switch is only working when the High/Variable switch is set at Variable settings. You can choose variable settings up to 10 different speed levels.

Operating Instructions

The Vitamix blender is specially designed for doing different tasks like mixing, blending, juice, soups, batters, sauces, frozen mixtures, wet chopping, and more. The following step-by-step operating information will help you to operate your Vitamix blender smoothly.

- **Wet Blade Container**
  1. First, place your Vitamix blender over a flat surface and plug the device into a power socket.
  2. Make sure the variable speed controller diet is set at 1 position.
  3. Before placing the container on the motor baseload it with liquid and soft foods. To get more precise blending results cut your ingredients and fruits into pieces before placing them into the container.
  4. After filling all the ingredients into the container close and lock the 2-part lid.
  5. Now place the wet blade container over the motor base and set it over the centering pad. Make sure the wet blade container is properly set and lock over the motor base.
  6. Set High/Variable switch on Variable position. Always start your blender at 1 variable position. Then push the ON/OFF switch at the ON position to start the blending process. Now slowly turn the variable speed dial to get the desire blending speed.
  7. Count the blending time to avoid over-processing your food.
  8. Then OFF the blender by pushing the ON/OFF switch at OFF position and wait till the blades stop completely. Then safely remove the container from the motor base.
  9. Now your wet blending food is ready.
- **Dry Blade Containers**
  1. First, place your Vitamix blender over a flat surface and plug the device into a power socket.
  2. Make sure the variable speed controller diet is set at 1 position.
  3. Now put the dry ingredients into a container and close and lock the 2-part lid.

4. Place the dry container over the motor base and set it over the centering pad. Make sure the wet blade container is properly set and lock over the motor base.

5. Set High/Variable switch on Variable position. Always start your blender at 1 variable position. Then push the ON/OFF switch at the ON position to start the blending process. Now slowly turn the variable speed dial to get the desire blending speed.

6. Count the blending time to avoid over-processing your food.

7. Do not grind dry ingredients over 2 minutes it may damage your blender.

8. Some herbs release the oil during dry grinding. It may be discoloring your container permanently. Grinding spices and herbs for a long time may cause to dull your dry grinding blade to dull because of overtime use.

9. Then OFF the blender by pushing the ON/OFF switch at OFF position and wait till the blades stop completely. Then safely remove the container from the motor base.

10. Now your dry grinding food is ready.

Advantages of Vitamix Blender

The Vitamix 5200 blender comes with various advantages some of them are mention as follows.

1. Make a healthy whole food meal under few minutes

The Vitamix 5200 blender is one of the flexible and versatile appliances ready to make juice, soups, and even fresh sorbet by just adding the frozen fruits and berries into a container with little water or you can use ice for optional. Process all these into a Vitamix container for few minutes and the healthy antioxidant-rich Sorbet is ready to serve.

2. Its Laser-cut blade is ready to break down tough seeds, skins, and stems

The Vitamix blenders work on 37000RPM with their sharpening blades. It crushes seeds, skins, and steam easily and makes your smoothie in few seconds. Add some vegetables and nuts like whole kale, carrot, pumpkin seeds, and spinach to process them within 30 to 60 seconds and your healthy smoothie is ready to serve.

3. Easy to operate

The Vitamix blenders come with three simple operating buttons in which two liver and one dial. The livers use to ON/OFF function and set High/Variable speed. The center-aligned variable speed dial is used to control the blender speed within 10 variable setting levels.

4. **You can cook food in a blender**

If you blend your food for a long and extended time it helps to cook soups, fondues, and syrups. There are no heating elements are present in the blender. It creates heat due to its high speed of blades. You just need to add some raw vegetables and water into a container and start the blending process your fresh hot soup is ready within three minutes.

5. **Easy to clean**

Don't forget to clean the blender after each use. Vitamix blender makes the cleaning process very simple. You just need to add some water with liquid detergent into a container and spin it at high settings for 30 seconds to 1 minute.

Cleaning and Maintenance

1. **Container**
   - Fill the container half with warm water and add few drops of liquid dishwasher into them.
   - Close and lock the 2-part lid over the container.
   - Place and lock the container over the motor base and set the variable controller at 1 position and start the blender.
   - Slowly increase the blender speed 1 to 10 and weight for 30 to 60 seconds at high speed.
   - Turn off the blender and rinse the water.
2. **Lid and Lid Plug**
   - Open and separate the lid and lid plug.
   - Wash it into soapy water
   - Hold and rinse it under running water and dry thoroughly.
   - Reassemble both the lid before use.
3. **Clean Motor Base**

- First, unplug the motor base from the power socket.
- Clean the motor base with the help of a damp cloth and sponge. Do not place the motor base into water.
- Remove the centering pad for thorough cleaning.
- Clean the switches properly with a soft damp cloth.

Chapter 2: Appetizers

Healthy Beetroot Dip

Preparation Time: 5 minutes
Cooking Time: 1 minute
Serve: 8

Ingredients:

- 1 cup pickled beets, drain the liquid
- 20 oz can white beans, drained
- 1 1/2 tbsp vinegar
- 1/4 cup olive oil
- 2 garlic cloves
- 3 tbsp fresh lemon juice
- 1 tbsp lemon zest
- 1/3 cup tahini
- 1/2 tsp salt

Directions:

1. Add all ingredients into the blender container. Secure the lid.
2. Start the blending at low speed, then quickly increase to highest speed and blend until smooth.
3. Serve and enjoy.

Nutritional Value (Amount per Serving):

- Calories 207
- Fat 11.9 g
- Carbohydrates 22.4 g
- Sugar 4.4 g
- Protein 7.2 g
- Cholesterol 0 mg

Flavorful Salsa Dip

Preparation Time: 5 minutes
Cooking Time: 1 minute
Serve: 10

Ingredients:

- 1 cup salsa
- 1 cup fresh cilantro
- 2 tsp taco seasoning
- 3/4 cup sour cream

Directions:

1. Add all ingredients into the blender container. Secure the lid.
2. Start the blending at low speed, then quickly increase to highest speed and blend until smooth.
3. Serve and enjoy.

Nutritional Value (Amount per Serving):

- Calories 119
- Fat 7.8 g
- Carbohydrates 7.8 g
- Sugar 0.8 g
- Protein 5.1 g
- Cholesterol 19 mg

Creamy Avocado Dip

Preparation Time: 5 minutes
Cooking Time: 1 minute
Serve: 6

Ingredients:

- 1 avocado, scoop out the flesh
- 1 lime juice
- 2 tbsp water
- 1 garlic clove
- 1/2 cup fresh cilantro
- 1/3 cup mayonnaise

Directions:

1. Add all ingredients into the blender container. Secure the lid.
2. Start the blending at low speed, then quickly increase to highest speed and blend until smooth.
3. Serve and enjoy.

Nutritional Value (Amount per Serving):

- Calories 122
- Fat 10.9 g
- Carbohydrates 6.8 g
- Sugar 1.2 g
- Protein 0.9 g
- Cholesterol 3 mg

Roasted Pepper Dip

Preparation Time: 5 minutes
Cooking Time: 1 minute
Serve: 12

Ingredients:

- 16 oz roasted red bell peppers, drained
- 1/4 tsp red pepper flakes
- 1 tsp paprika
- 1 tbsp honey
- 1 tbsp lime juice
- 1 tbsp extra-virgin olive oil
- 2 garlic cloves
- 1 1/2 cups walnuts, roasted
- Salt

Directions:

1. Add all ingredients into the blender container. Secure the lid.
2. Start the blending at low speed, then quickly increase to highest speed and blend until smooth.
3. Serve and enjoy.

Nutritional Value (Amount per Serving):

- Calories 138
- Fat 12.2 g
- Carbohydrates 7.1 g
- Sugar 2.9 g
- Protein 5 g
- Cholesterol 0 mg

Creamy Feta Dip

Preparation Time: 5 minutes
Cooking Time: 1 minute
Serve: 4

Ingredients:

- 7 oz feta cheese, drained
- 1/2 tsp lemon zest
- 1 tbsp olive oil
- 1/2 cup sour cream
- Pepper
- Salt

Directions:

1. Add all ingredients into the blender container. Secure the lid.
2. Start the blending at low speed, then quickly increase to highest speed and blend until smooth & creamy.
3. Serve and enjoy.

Nutritional Value (Amount per Serving):

- Calories 223
- Fat 20.1 g
- Carbohydrates 3.3 g
- Sugar 2.1 g
- Protein 8 g
- Cholesterol 57 mg

Quick Olive Dip

Preparation Time: 5 minutes
Cooking Time: 1 minute
Serve: 8

Ingredients:

- 6 oz green olives, drained
- 16 oz cream cheese, softened
- 1/2 tsp garlic powder
- 1/2 tsp onion powder
- 1/2 cup mayonnaise

Directions:

1. Add all ingredients into the blender container. Secure the lid.
2. Start the blending at low speed, then quickly increase to highest speed and blend for 1 minute or until getting the desired consistency.
3. Serve and enjoy.

Nutritional Value (Amount per Serving):

- Calories 274
- Fat 26.1 g
- Carbohydrates 6.5 g
- Sugar 1.1 g
- Protein 4.7 g
- Cholesterol 66 mg

Feta Red Pepper Dip

Preparation Time: 5 minutes
Cooking Time: 1 minute
Serve: 8

Ingredients:

- 1/2 cup can roasted red peppers, drained
- 8 oz feta cheese
- 1/3 cup extra-virgin olive oil
- 4 garlic cloves
- Pepper
- Salt

Directions:

1. Add all ingredients into the blender container. Secure the lid.
2. Start the blending at low speed, then quickly increase to highest speed and blend until smooth.
3. Serve and enjoy.

Nutritional Value (Amount per Serving):

- Calories 155
- Fat 14.6 g
- Carbohydrates 2.8 g
- Sugar 1.9 g
- Protein 4.3 g
- Cholesterol 25 mg

Creamy Spinach Dip

Preparation Time: 5 minutes
Cooking Time: 1 minute
Serve: 12

Ingredients:

- 10 oz frozen spinach, thawed & drained
- 1/2 tsp garlic powder
- 1/4 tsp cayenne
- 8 oz sour cream
- 1 tbsp fresh lime juice

Directions:

1. Add all ingredients into the blender container. Secure the lid.
2. Start the blending at low speed, then quickly increase to highest speed and blend until smooth.
3. Serve and enjoy.

Nutritional Value (Amount per Serving):

- Calories 339
- Fat 10 g
- Carbohydrates 56.1 g
- Sugar 22 g
- Protein 7.5 g
- Cholesterol 76 mg

Tomato Chickpeas Hummus

Preparation Time: 5 minutes
Cooking Time: 1 minute
Serve: 8

Ingredients:

- 14 oz can chickpeas, drained & rinsed
- 1/2 tsp onion powder
- 1/2 tsp dried basil
- 1/2 tsp dried oregano
- 2 tbsp fresh lime juice
- 2 garlic cloves
- 1/4 cup tahini
- 1/3 cup aquafaba
- 1/3 cup sun-dried tomatoes
- Pepper
- Salt

Directions:

1. Add all ingredients into the blender container. Secure the lid.
2. Start the blending at low speed, then quickly increase to highest speed and blend until smooth.
3. Serve and enjoy.

Nutritional Value (Amount per Serving):

- Calories 110
- Fat 4.6 g
- Carbohydrates 14.5 g
- Sugar 0.5 g
- Protein 3.9 g
- Cholesterol 0 mg

Easy Jalapeno Ranch Dip

Preparation Time: 5 minutes
Cooking Time: 1 minute
Serve: 4

Ingredients:

- 8 oz can jalapeno peppers with juice
- 1 cup sour cream
- 1 cup mayonnaise
- 1/2 tsp garlic powder
- 1/4 cup fresh cilantro
- 1/2 tsp pepper
- 1 tsp salt

Directions:

1. Add all ingredients into the blender container. Secure the lid.
2. Start the blending at low speed, then quickly increase to highest speed and blend until smooth.
3. Serve and enjoy.

Nutritional Value (Amount per Serving):

- Calories 354
- Fat 31.7 g
- Carbohydrates 17 g
- Sugar 4 g
- Protein 2.5 g
- Cholesterol 41 mg

Roasted Pepper Hummus

Preparation Time: 5 minutes
Cooking Time: 1 minute
Serve: 8

Ingredients:

- 15 oz can chickpeas, drain
- 1 tsp ground cumin
- 4 garlic cloves
- 1 tbsp tahini
- 1/4 cup fresh lemon juice
- 1/2 cup roasted red peppers, drained
- 1/4 cup vegetable broth
- Pepper
- Salt

Directions:

1. Add all ingredients into the blender container. Secure the lid.
2. Start the blending at low speed, then quickly increase to highest speed and blend until smooth.
3. Serve and enjoy.

Nutritional Value (Amount per Serving):

- Calories 83
- Fat 1.8 g
- Carbohydrates 13.8 g
- Sugar 0.7 g
- Protein 3.4 g
- Cholesterol 0 mg

Spicy Chipotle Ranch Dip

Preparation Time: 5 minutes
Cooking Time: 1 minute
Serve: 4

Ingredients:

- 2 chipotle peppers in adobo sauce
- 3 tbsp water
- 1 garlic clove
- 1/2 tbsp fresh lime juice
- 1 tsp dried dill
- 1/2 tsp onion powder
- 1 1/2 tsp garlic powder
- 1/2 cup Greek yogurt
- 1/2 cup mayonnaise
- Pepper
- Salt

Directions:

1. Add all ingredients into the blender container. Secure the lid.
2. Start the blending at low speed, then quickly increase to highest speed and blend until smooth.
3. Serve and enjoy.

Nutritional Value (Amount per Serving):

- Calories 154
- Fat 10.6 g
- Carbohydrates 12.9 g
- Sugar 4.4 g
- Protein 3.1 g
- Cholesterol 9 mg

Cannellini Bean Dip

Preparation Time: 5 minutes
Cooking Time: 1 minute
Serve: 8

Ingredients:

- 1 cup can cannellini beans, drained
- 4 tbsp tahini
- 1 lemon juice
- 1 1/2 tsp ground cumin
- 1/4 cup olive oil
- 1/4 cup water
- 2 garlic cloves
- 1 cup can chickpeas, drained
- Salt

Directions:

1. Add all ingredients into the blender container. Secure the lid.
2. Start the blending at low speed, then quickly increase to highest speed and blend until smooth.
3. Serve and enjoy.

Nutritional Value (Amount per Serving):

- Calories 168
- Fat 10.8 g
- Carbohydrates 14.2 g
- Sugar 0.4 g
- Protein 4.9 g
- Cholesterol 0 mg

Cashew Queso Dip

Preparation Time: 5 minutes
Cooking Time: 1 minute
Serve: 8

Ingredients:

- 1 cup cashews
- 1/2 tsp chili powder
- 1 garlic clove
- 1/2 tsp paprika
- 1 tsp onion powder
- 1/3 cup marinara sauce
- 3/4 cup hot water
- Pepper
- Salt

Directions:

1. Add all ingredients into the blender container. Secure the lid.
2. Start the blending at low speed, then quickly increase to highest speed and blend until smooth.
3. Serve and enjoy.

Nutritional Value (Amount per Serving):

- Calories 110
- Fat 8.3 g
- Carbohydrates 7.6 g
- Sugar 1.9 g
- Protein 2.9 g
- Cholesterol 0 mg

Perfect Artichoke Dip

Preparation Time: 5 minutes
Cooking Time: 1 minute
Serve: 4

Ingredients:

- 14 oz can artichoke hearts, drained
- 2 tbsp water
- 1 tsp chili powder
- 2 garlic cloves
- 1 tbsp lemon juice
- 2 tbsp olive oil
- 2 tbsp tahini
- 1/4 cup nutritional yeast
- 15 oz can chickpeas, drained
- Pepper
- Salt

Directions:

1. Add all ingredients into the blender container. Secure the lid.
2. Start the blending at low speed, then quickly increase to highest speed and blend for 1 minute or until getting the desired consistency.
3. Serve and enjoy.

Nutritional Value (Amount per Serving):

- Calories 301
- Fat 12.9 g
- Carbohydrates 36.1 g
- Sugar 1 g
- Protein 13 g
- Cholesterol 0 mg

Curried Cashew Dip

Preparation Time: 5 minutes
Cooking Time: 1 minute
Serve: 8

Ingredients:

- 1 cup cashews
- 1/8 tsp white pepper
- 1/8 tsp garlic powder
- 1/8 tsp cayenne
- 1/2 tsp curry powder
- 1 lemon zest
- 3 tbsp fresh lemon juice
- 1/3 cup full-fat coconut milk
- 3/4 cup mayonnaise
- Salt

Directions:

1. Add all ingredients into the blender container. Secure the lid.
2. Start the blending at low speed, then quickly increase to highest speed and blend until smooth.
3. Serve and enjoy.

Nutritional Value (Amount per Serving):

- Calories 257
- Fat 22.6 g
- Carbohydrates 13.5 g
- Sugar 3.6 g
- Protein 3.7 g
- Cholesterol 6 mg

Flavorful Cranberry Salsa

Preparation Time: 5 minutes
Cooking Time: 1 minute
Serve: 8

Ingredients:

- 12 oz fresh cranberries
- 2 jalapeno peppers, chopped
- 1/4 cup fresh cilantro
- 1 tbsp orange zest
- 2 tbsp ginger, chopped
- 2 tbsp fresh lemon juice
- 1/2 cup sugar
- Pinch of salt

Directions:

1. Add all ingredients into the blender container. Secure the lid.
2. Start the blending at low speed, then quickly increase to highest speed and blend until getting chunky consistency.
3. Pour blended mixture into the bowl and place in the refrigerator for 5-6 hours.
4. Serve and enjoy.

Nutritional Value (Amount per Serving):

- Calories 78
- Fat 0.2 g
- Carbohydrates 17.9 g
- Sugar 14.3 g
- Protein 0.2 g
- Cholesterol 0 mg

Easy Olive Tapenade

Preparation Time: 5 minutes
Cooking Time: 1 minute
Serve: 4

Ingredients:

- 2 cups olives, pitted
- 1/4 cup olive oil
- 1 tbsp fresh lemon juice
- 2 tbsp parsley
- 1 tbsp fresh basil
- 2 garlic cloves
- 1 tbsp capers
- 1/4 cup sun-dried tomatoes, drained

Directions:

1. Add all ingredients into the blender container. Secure the lid.
2. Start the blending at low speed, then quickly increase to highest speed and blend for 1 minute or until getting the desired consistency.
3. Serve and enjoy.

Nutritional Value (Amount per Serving):

- Calories 192
- Fat 19.9 g
- Carbohydrates 5.5 g
- Sugar 0.4 g
- Protein 0.9 g
- Cholesterol 0 mg

Avocado Salsa Dip

Preparation Time: 5 minutes
Cooking Time: 1 minute
Serve: 12

Ingredients:

- 2 avocados, scoop out the flesh
- 1/4 tsp ground cumin
- 1/2 tsp garlic powder
- 1 garlic clove
- 1/3 cup onion, chopped
- 1/2 cup cilantro
- 1 lime juice
- 1 jalapeno pepper
- 10 oz tomatillos
- Salt

Directions:

1. Add all ingredients into the blender container. Secure the lid.
2. Start the blending at low speed, then quickly increase to highest speed and blend for 1 minute or until getting the desired consistency.
3. Serve and enjoy.

Nutritional Value (Amount per Serving):

- Calories 80
- Fat 6.8 g
- Carbohydrates 5.2 g
- Sugar 0.5 g
- Protein 1 g
- Cholesterol 0 mg

Lemon Pepper Cheese Dip

Preparation Time: 5 minutes
Cooking Time: 1 minute
Serve: 8

Ingredients:

- 4 oz Asiago cheese, cubed
- 1/2 lemon juice
- 1 lemon zest
- 2 garlic cloves
- 1 tbsp thyme, minced
- 6 tbsp sour cream
- 1 oz parmesan cheese
- 1/2 tsp pepper
- 1/4 tsp salt

Directions:

1. Add all ingredients into the blender container. Secure the lid.
2. Start the blending at low speed, then quickly increase to highest speed and blend until smooth.
3. Serve and enjoy.

Nutritional Value (Amount per Serving):

- Calories 85
- Fat 6.8 g
- Carbohydrates 1.2 g
- Sugar 0.1 g
- Protein 5.1 g
- Cholesterol 19 mg

Lemon Garlic Pistachio Dip

Preparation Time: 5 minutes
Cooking Time: 1 minute
Serve: 8

Ingredients:

- 1/4 cup pistachios
- 1 cup shelled edamame, cooked
- 1/2 cup water
- 2 tbsp olive oil
- 1 fresh lemon juice
- 1 garlic clove
- 1/2 cup fresh parsley
- Pepper
- Salt

Directions:

1. Add all ingredients into the blender container. Secure the lid.
2. Start the blending at low speed, then quickly increase to highest speed and blend for 1 minute or until getting the desired consistency.
3. Serve and enjoy.

Nutritional Value (Amount per Serving):

- Calories 64
- Fat 5.4 g
- Carbohydrates 2.4 g
- Sugar 0.6 g
- Protein 2.3 g
- Cholesterol 0 mg

Easy Avocado Dip

Preparation Time: 5 minutes
Cooking Time: 1 minute
Serve: 6

Ingredients:

- 2 avocados, scoop out the flesh
- 1/4 tsp onion powder
- 1/2 cup Greek yogurt
- 1 lemon juice
- 1 cup fresh cilantro
- 2 garlic cloves
- Pepper
- Salt

Directions:

1. Add all ingredients into the blender container. Secure the lid.
2. Start the blending at low speed, then quickly increase to highest speed and blend until smooth.
3. Serve and enjoy.

Nutritional Value (Amount per Serving):

- Calories 154
- Fat 13.5 g
- Carbohydrates 7.1 g
- Sugar 1.2 g
- Protein 3.1 g
- Cholesterol 1 mg

Corn Salsa

Preparation Time: 5 minutes
Cooking Time: 1 minute
Serve: 4

Ingredients:

- 1 cup corn kernels, thawed
- 1/2 cup scallions, chopped
- 1 lime juice
- 1 jalapeno, chopped
- 1/4 cup fresh cilantro
- 2 small tomatoes, chopped
- Salt

Directions:

1. Add all ingredients into the blender container. Secure the lid.
2. Start the blending at low speed, then quickly increase to highest speed and blend until getting chunky consistency.
3. Serve and enjoy.

Nutritional Value (Amount per Serving):

- Calories 49
- Fat 0.6 g
- Carbohydrates 11.1 g
- Sugar 3.1 g
- Protein 2 g
- Cholesterol 0 mg

Cauliflower Artichoke Dip

Preparation Time: 5 minutes
Cooking Time: 1 minute
Serve: 8

Ingredients:

- 2 cups artichoke hearts
- 1/2 cup cauliflower florets, cooked
- 3 cups spinach, chopped
- 2 tsp nutritional yeast
- 1/3 cup vegetable broth
- 1/2 cup coconut cream, softened
- 3 garlic cloves, minced
- 1 onion, diced
- 2 tbsp olive oil
- 1 tsp salt

Directions:

1. Add all ingredients into the blender container. Secure the lid.
2. Start the blending at low speed, then quickly increase to highest speed and blend for 1 minute or until getting the desired consistency.
3. Serve and enjoy.

Nutritional Value (Amount per Serving):

- Calories 95
- Fat 7.3 g
- Carbohydrates 7 g
- Sugar 1.6 g
- Protein 2.6 g
- Cholesterol 0 mg

Quick & Easy Black Bean Dip

Preparation Time: 5 minutes
Cooking Time: 1 minute
Serve: 8

Ingredients:

- 30 oz can black beans, drained
- 1/4 tsp onion powder
- 1/4 tsp smoked paprika
- 1/4 tsp ground cumin
- 1/2 tsp chili powder
- 1 1/2 tsp garlic, minced
- 1 tbsp fresh lime juice
- 1/2 cup fire-roasted tomatoes, diced
- 1/2 tsp salt

Directions:

1. Add all ingredients into the blender container. Secure the lid.
2. Start the blending at low speed, then quickly increase to highest speed and blend for 1 minute or until getting the desired consistency.
3. Serve and enjoy.

Nutritional Value (Amount per Serving):

- Calories 105
- Fat 0.8 g
- Carbohydrates 19.7 g
- Sugar 1.2 g
- Protein 5.8 g
- Cholesterol 0 mg

Chapter 3: Soups & Salsas

Tomato Pepper Soup

Preparation Time: 5 minutes
Cooking Time: 6 minutes
Serve: 4

Ingredients:

- 1 lb fresh tomatoes, halved
- 3 garlic cloves
- 2 cups vegetable stock
- 14 oz can tomatoes
- 1 onion, sliced
- 2 peppers, sliced
- 1 tbsp olive oil
- 1 1/2 tsp red chili flakes
- Pepper
- Salt

Directions:

1. Add all ingredients into the blender container. Secure the lid.
2. Start the blending at low speed, then quickly increase to highest speed and blend for 6 minutes.
3. Serve and enjoy.

Nutritional Value (Amount per Serving):

- Calories 90
- Fat 3.8 g
- Carbohydrates 13.6 g
- Sugar 7.9 g
- Protein 2.6 g
- Cholesterol 0 mg

Cauliflower Soup

Preparation Time: 5 minutes
Cooking Time: 6 minutes
Serve: 4

Ingredients:

- 2 cups cauliflower florets, boiled & drained
- 1 tsp pumpkin pie spice
- 1 onion, chopped
- 5 cups vegetable broth
- 3 tbsp olive oil
- Pepper
- Salt

Directions:

1. Add all ingredients into the blender container. Secure the lid.
2. Start the blending at low speed, then quickly increase to highest speed and blend for 6 minutes.
3. Serve and enjoy.

Nutritional Value (Amount per Serving):

- Calories 163
- Fat 12.3 g
- Carbohydrates 6.7 g
- Sugar 3.3 g
- Protein 7.4 g
- Cholesterol 0 mg

Creamy Squash Soup

Preparation Time: 5 minutes
Cooking Time: 6 minutes
Serve: 6

Ingredients:

- 6 cups butternut squash, peel, cook, and cubed
- 2 tsp thyme
- 1/4 cup heavy cream
- 3 cups vegetable stock
- 1 onion, chopped
- 1/8 tsp nutmeg
- 2 tbsp olive oil
- 1/8 tsp cayenne
- Pepper
- Salt

Directions:

1. Add all ingredients into the blender container. Secure the lid.
2. Start the blending at low speed, then quickly increase to highest speed and blend for 6 minutes.
3. Serve and enjoy.

Nutritional Value (Amount per Serving):

- Calories 132
- Fat 6.8 g
- Carbohydrates 18.9 g
- Sugar 4.2 g
- Protein 1.9 g
- Cholesterol 7 mg

Creamy Asparagus Soup

Preparation Time: 5 minutes
Cooking Time: 6 minutes
Serve: 4

Ingredients:

- 1 lb asparagus, cooked and chopped
- 2 garlic cloves
- 1 onion, diced
- 3 1/4 cups vegetable stock
- 1 tbsp olive oil
- 1 tbsp fresh lemon juice
- 1 leek, sliced
- Pepper
- Salt

Directions:

1. Add all ingredients into the blender container. Secure the lid.
2. Start the blending at low speed, then quickly increase to highest speed and blend for 6 minutes.
3. Serve and enjoy.

Nutritional Value (Amount per Serving):

- Calories 85
- Fat 3.9 g
- Carbohydrates 11.5 g
- Sugar 4.8 g
- Protein 3.6 g
- Cholesterol 0 mg

Spicy Squash Soup

Preparation Time: 5 minutes
Cooking Time: 6 minutes
Serve: 4

Ingredients:

- 1 butternut squash, cut into chunks
- 1 potato, peel, cook, and chopped
- 1 onion, chopped
- 1 red chili, chopped
- 3 garlic cloves, peeled
- 3 cups vegetable stock
- Pepper
- Salt

Directions:

1. Add all ingredients into the blender container. Secure the lid.
2. Start the blending at low speed, then quickly increase to highest speed and blend for 6 minutes.
3. Serve and enjoy.

Nutritional Value (Amount per Serving):

- Calories 68
- Fat 0.2 g
- Carbohydrates 15.6 g
- Sugar 2.9 g
- Protein 2 g
- Cholesterol 0 mg

Tomatillo Pineapple Salsa

Preparation Time: 5 minutes
Cooking Time: 1 minute
Serve: 8

Ingredients:

- 1 cup pineapple, diced
- 1 jalapeno pepper
- 1 lb tomatillos, husks removed & chopped
- 1 cup water
- 1/2 lime juice
- 1/2 cup cilantro
- 4.5 green chilies, diced
- 1/2 onion, chopped
- 1/2 tsp salt

Directions:

1. Add all ingredients into the blender container. Secure the lid.
2. Start the blending at low speed, then slowly increase speed to variable 3 and blend for 15-20 seconds or until getting the desired consistency.
3. Serve and enjoy.

Nutritional Value (Amount per Serving):

- Calories 34
- Fat 0.7 g
- Carbohydrates 7.2 g
- Sugar 2.6 g
- Protein 0.8 g
- Cholesterol 0 mg

Tasty Garden Salsa

Preparation Time: 5 minutes
Cooking Time: 1 minute
Serve: 8

Ingredients:

- 5 tomatoes, halved
- 2 garlic cloves
- 1 lime juice
- 1 jalapeno pepper
- 1/2 onion
- 1/2 tsp sugar
- Pepper
- Salt

Directions:

1. Add all ingredients into the blender container. Secure the lid.
2. Start the blending at low speed, then slowly increase speed to variable 3 and blend for 15-20 seconds or until getting the desired consistency.
3. Serve and enjoy.

Nutritional Value (Amount per Serving):

- Calories 21
- Fat 0.2 g
- Carbohydrates 4.7 g
- Sugar 2.7 g
- Protein 0.9 g
- Cholesterol 0 mg

Mango Salsa

Preparation Time: 5 minutes
Cooking Time: 1 minute
Serve: 8

Ingredients:

- 1 1/2 cups mangoes, diced
- 1/3 cup green onion, chopped
- 1 bell pepper, diced
- 1 lime juice
- 1 jalapeno pepper, diced
- 1/2 cup cilantro
- Salt

Directions:

1. Add all ingredients into the blender container. Secure the lid.
2. Start the blending at low speed, then slowly increase speed to variable 3 and blend for 15-20 seconds or until getting the desired consistency.
3. Serve and enjoy.

Nutritional Value (Amount per Serving):

- Calories 25
- Fat 0.2 g
- Carbohydrates 6.7 g
- Sugar 5.2 g
- Protein 0.5 g
- Cholesterol 0 mg

Strawberry Salsa

Preparation Time: 5 minutes
Cooking Time: 1 minute
Serve: 4

Ingredients:

- 1 cup strawberries
- 1/4 cup cilantro
- 1 lime juice
- 1 jalapeno pepper
- 1/4 onion

Directions:

1. Add all ingredients into the blender container. Secure the lid.
2. Start the blending at low speed, then slowly increase speed to variable 3 and blend for 15-20 seconds or until getting chunky consistency.
3. Serve and enjoy.

Nutritional Value (Amount per Serving):

- Calories 18
- Fat 0.2 g
- Carbohydrates 4.6 g
- Sugar 2.4 g
- Protein 0.4 g
- Cholesterol 0 mg

Delicious Cranberry Salsa

Preparation Time: 5 minutes
Cooking Time: 1 minute
Serve: 8

Ingredients:

- 12 oz cranberries
- 2 jalapeno pepper, chopped
- 1/4 cup cilantro
- 1 tbsp lemon zest
- 1 1/2 tbsp ginger, chopped
- 2 tbsp lime juice
- 1/2 cup sugar

Directions:

1. Add all ingredients into the blender container. Secure the lid.
2. Start the blending at low speed, then slowly increase speed to variable 3 and blend for 15-20 seconds or until getting the desired consistency.
3. Serve and enjoy.

Nutritional Value (Amount per Serving):

- Calories 78
- Fat 0.1 g
- Carbohydrates 18.4 g
- Sugar 14.2 g
- Protein 0.2 g
- Cholesterol 0 mg

Berry Salsa

Preparation Time: 5 minutes
Cooking Time: 1 minute
Serve: 8

Ingredients:

- 8 strawberries
- 2 cups blueberries
- 1 lime juice
- 1 jalapeno pepper
- 1/4 cup cilantro
- Salt

Directions:

1. Add all ingredients into the blender container. Secure the lid.
2. Start the blending at low speed, then slowly increase speed to variable 3 and blend for 15-20 seconds or until getting the desired consistency.
3. Serve and enjoy.

Nutritional Value (Amount per Serving):

- Calories 25
- Fat 0.2 g
- Carbohydrates 6.3 g
- Sugar 4.3 g
- Protein 0.4 g
- Cholesterol 0 mg

Broccoli Soup

Preparation Time: 5 minutes
Cooking Time: 6 minutes
Serve: 4

Ingredients:

- 4 cups broccoli florets, boil & drained
- 3 garlic cloves
- 6 cup vegetable stock
- 1 tsp thyme
- 1 potato, peel, cooked, and cubed
- 1/2 tsp onion powder
- Pepper
- Salt

Directions:

1. Add all ingredients into the blender container. Secure the lid.
2. Start the blending at low speed, then quickly increase to highest speed and blend for 6 minutes.
3. Serve and enjoy.

Nutritional Value (Amount per Serving):

- Calories 78
- Fat 0.5 g
- Carbohydrates 16 g
- Sugar 3.1 g
- Protein 4.2 g
- Cholesterol 0 mg

Potato Leek Soup

Preparation Time: 5 minutes
Cooking Time: 6 minutes
Serve: 4

Ingredients:

- 1 lb potatoes, peel, cooked, and chopped
- 1 onion, chopped
- 1 cup leek, chopped
- 3 cups vegetable stock
- 1/2 cup fresh cream
- Pepper
- Salt

Directions:

1. Add all ingredients into the blender container. Secure the lid.
2. Start the blending at low speed, then quickly increase to highest speed and blend for 6 minutes.
3. Serve and enjoy.

Nutritional Value (Amount per Serving):

- Calories 127
- Fat 2 g
- Carbohydrates 25.2 g
- Sugar 4.5 g
- Protein 3.1 g
- Cholesterol 6 mg

Easy Onion Soup

Preparation Time: 5 minutes
Cooking Time: 6 minutes
Serve: 6

Ingredients:

- 8 cups onions, peel and slice
- 6 cups vegetable broth
- 2 tbsp olive oil
- 1/4 tsp garlic powder
- 1 tbsp balsamic vinegar
- Pepper
- Salt

Directions:

1. Add all ingredients into the blender container. Secure the lid.
2. Start the blending at low speed, then quickly increase to highest speed and blend for 6 minutes.
3. Serve and enjoy.

Nutritional Value (Amount per Serving):

- Calories 141
- Fat 6.2 g
- Carbohydrates 15.4 g
- Sugar 7.2 g
- Protein 6.6 g
- Cholesterol 0 mg

Spicy Chipotle Salsa

Preparation Time: 5 minutes
Cooking Time: 1 minute
Serve: 8

Ingredients:

- 10 oz can tomatoes with green chilies
- 14 oz can tomatoes, diced
- 4 garlic cloves
- 1 small onion, diced
- 1 tsp ground cumin
- 1 tbsp lime juice
- 2 chipotle peppers
- 1/2 cup cilantro
- Salt

Directions:

1. Add all ingredients into the blender container. Secure the lid.
2. Start the blending at low speed, then slowly increase speed to variable 3 and blend for 15-20 seconds or until getting the desired consistency.
3. Serve and enjoy.

Nutritional Value (Amount per Serving):

- Calories 29
- Fat 0.1 g
- Carbohydrates 6.8 g
- Sugar 2.8 g
- Protein 1.2 g
- Cholesterol 0 mg

Chapter 4: Dressing, Sauces & Spreads

Chipotle Sauce

Preparation Time: 10 minutes
Cooking Time: 1 minute
Serve: 10

Ingredients:

- 7 oz can chipotle peppers in adobo sauce
- 1/2 cup cilantro
- 3/4 tsp garlic powder
- 1 tsp ground cumin
- 1 tsp chili powder
- 4 tbsp mayonnaise
- 1/2 cup Greek yogurt
- Salt

Directions:

1. Add all ingredients into the blender container. Secure the lid.
2. Start the blending at low speed, then quickly increase to highest speed and blend for 1 minute or until smooth.
3. Serve and enjoy.

Nutritional Value (Amount per Serving):

- Calories 53
- Fat 3.2 g
- Carbohydrates 4.9 g
- Sugar 2.8 g
- Protein 1.9 g
- Cholesterol 2 mg

Chimichurri Sauce

Preparation Time: 10 minutes
Cooking Time: 1 minute
Serve: 8

Ingredients:

- 1 jalapeno pepper
- 1 small onion, quartered
- 4 garlic cloves
- 2 tsp dried oregano
- 1/2 cup fresh cilantro
- 1/2 cup fresh parsley
- 1/2 cup vinegar
- 1/2 cup extra-virgin olive oil
- Pepper
- Salt

Directions:

1. Add all ingredients into the blender container. Secure the lid.
2. Start the blending at low speed, then quickly increase to highest speed and blend for 1 minute or until smooth.
3. Serve and enjoy.

Nutritional Value (Amount per Serving):

- Calories 120
- Fat 12.7 g
- Carbohydrates 2.1 g
- Sugar 0.6 g
- Protein 0.4 g
- Cholesterol 0 mg

Enchilada Sauce

Preparation Time: 10 minutes
Cooking Time: 1 minute
Serve: 4

Ingredients:

- 8 oz can tomato sauce
- 1/4 tsp cayenne
- 1/4 tsp garlic powder
- 1/4 tsp ground cumin
- 1 cup water
- 2 tbsp chili powder
- 2 tbsp flour
- 1/4 cup olive oil
- Pepper
- Salt

Directions:

1. Add all ingredients into the blender container. Secure the lid.
2. Start the blending at low speed, then quickly increase to highest speed and blend for 1 minute or until smooth.
3. Serve and enjoy.

Nutritional Value (Amount per Serving):

- Calories 149
- Fat 13.4 g
- Carbohydrates 8.4 g
- Sugar 2.7 g
- Protein 1.7 g
- Cholesterol 0 mg

Zesty Chipotle Ranch Dressing

Preparation Time: 10 minutes
Cooking Time: 1 minute
Serve: 6

Ingredients:

- 1 chipotle pepper
- 1/2 tsp dill
- 1/4 tsp onion powder
- 1/2 tsp garlic powder
- 2 tbsp cilantro
- 1 tbsp lime juice
- 1/4 cup buttermilk
- 1/4 cup sour cream
- 1/2 cup mayonnaise
- Pepper
- Salt

Directions:

1. Add all ingredients into the blender container. Secure the lid.
2. Start the blending at low speed, then quickly increase to highest speed and blend for 1 minute or until smooth.
3. Serve and enjoy.

Nutritional Value (Amount per Serving):

- Calories 111
- Fat 8.7 g
- Carbohydrates 8.1 g
- Sugar 2.8 g
- Protein 1.3 g
- Cholesterol 10 mg

Low-carb BBQ Sauce

Preparation Time: 10 minutes
Cooking Time: 1 minute
Serve: 4

Ingredients:

- 6 oz can tomato paste
- 1 tsp Dijon mustard
- 1/2 tsp chipotle powder
- 3/4 tsp paprika
- 1 tsp garlic powder
- 1 tbsp onion powder
- 1/2 cup Swerve
- 2 tbsp water
- 1/4 cup vinegar
- 1 tsp salt

Directions:

1. Add all ingredients into the blender container. Secure the lid.
2. Start the blending at low speed, then quickly increase to highest speed and blend for 1 minute or until smooth.
3. Serve and enjoy.

Nutritional Value (Amount per Serving):

- Calories 49
- Fat 0.4 g
- Carbohydrates 10.6 g
- Sugar 6.1 g
- Protein 2.3 g
- Cholesterol 0 mg

Creamy Avocado Dressing

Preparation Time: 10 minutes
Cooking Time: 1 minute
Serve: 4

Ingredients:

- 1 avocado, scoop out the flesh
- 1 garlic clove
- 1 lemon juice
- 2 tbsp water
- 1/4 cup olive oil
- 1/2 cup cilantro
- Pepper
- Salt

Directions:

1. Add all ingredients into the blender container. Secure the lid.
2. Start the blending at low speed, then quickly increase to highest speed and blend for 1 minute or until smooth.
3. Serve and enjoy.

Nutritional Value (Amount per Serving):

- Calories 215
- Fat 22.5 g
- Carbohydrates 4.9 g
- Sugar 0.5 g
- Protein 1.1 g
- Cholesterol 0 mg

Classic French Dressing

Preparation Time: 10 minutes
Cooking Time: 1 minute
Serve: 6

Ingredients:

- 1/2 cup olive oil
- 1/2 tsp maple syrup
- 1 garlic clove
- 1 tsp Dijon mustard
- 1 tbsp lemon juice
- 2 tbsp parsley
- 2 tbsp vinegar
- Pepper
- Salt

Directions:

1. Add all ingredients into the blender container. Secure the lid.
2. Start the blending at low speed, then quickly increase to highest speed and blend for 1 minute or until smooth.
3. Serve and enjoy.

Nutritional Value (Amount per Serving):

- Calories 149
- Fat 16.9 g
- Carbohydrates 0.8 g
- Sugar 0.4 g
- Protein 0.1 g
- Cholesterol 0 mg

Creamy Avocado Sauce

Preparation Time: 10 minutes
Cooking Time: 1 minute
Serve: 8

Ingredients:

- 1 avocado, scoop out the flesh
- 2 tbsp fresh lemon juice
- 4 oz sour cream
- 1/4 tsp garlic powder
- Pepper
- Salt

Directions:

1. Add all ingredients into the blender container. Secure the lid.
2. Start the blending at low speed, then quickly increase to highest speed and blend for 1 minute or until smooth.
3. Serve and enjoy.

Nutritional Value (Amount per Serving):

- Calories 83
- Fat 7.9 g
- Carbohydrates 2.9 g
- Sugar 0.3 g
- Protein 1 g
- Cholesterol 6 mg

Southwest Dressing

Preparation Time: 10 minutes
Cooking Time: 1 minute
Serve: 8

Ingredients:

- 1/4 tsp chipotle powder
- 1/2 tsp paprika
- 1/2 tsp dill
- 1 tsp ground cumin
- 1 tsp onion powder
- 1 tsp garlic powder
- 1 1/2 tsp chili powder
- 1/4 cup fresh lemon juice
- 1 cup mayonnaise
- Salt

Directions:

1. Add all ingredients into the blender container. Secure the lid.
2. Start the blending at low speed, then quickly increase to highest speed and blend for 1 minute or until smooth.
3. Serve and enjoy.

Nutritional Value (Amount per Serving):

- Calories 138
- Fat 11.8 g
- Carbohydrates 8.3 g
- Sugar 2.4 g
- Protein 0.6 g
- Cholesterol 9 mg

Chickpea Pepper Spread

Preparation Time: 10 minutes
Cooking Time: 1 minute
Serve: 8

Ingredients:

- 14.5 oz can chickpeas, drained
- 1 tbsp olive oil
- 1/2 tsp paprika
- 1 tbsp vinegar
- 4 oz can roasted red peppers, drained
- Pepper
- Salt

Directions:

1. Add all ingredients into the blender container. Secure the lid.
2. Start the blending at low speed, then quickly increase to highest speed and blend for 1 minute or until smooth & creamy.
3. Serve and enjoy.

Nutritional Value (Amount per Serving):

- Calories 83
- Fat 2.5 g
- Carbohydrates 12.7 g
- Sugar 0.6 g
- Protein 2.7 g
- Cholesterol 0 mg

Vegan Greek Dressing

Preparation Time: 10 minutes
Cooking Time: 1 minute
Serve: 8

Ingredients:

- 1 cup olive oil
- 1/4 tsp red chili flakes
- 1/4 cup parsley
- 1 tbsp Dijon mustard
- 1 tsp dried basil
- 1 tsp dried oregano
- 2 garlic cloves
- 1/3 cup water
- 1/2 cup vinegar
- Pepper
- Salt

Directions:

1. Add all ingredients into the blender container. Secure the lid.
2. Start the blending at low speed, then quickly increase to highest speed and blend for 1 minute or until smooth.
3. Serve and enjoy.

Nutritional Value (Amount per Serving):

- Calories 223
- Fat 25.3 g
- Carbohydrates 0.7 g
- Sugar 0.1 g
- Protein 0.2 g
- Cholesterol 0 mg

Delicious Sandwich Spread

Preparation Time: 10 minutes
Cooking Time: 1 minute
Serve: 8

Ingredients:

- 1/3 cup tahini
- 2 tbsp nutritional yeast
- 14.5 oz can chickpeas, drained
- 1 carrot, peeled & diced
- 2 kale leaves
- 1/2 tsp ground cumin
- 1/2 tsp curry powder
- 2 tsp mustard
- 2 tbsp lime juice
- 2 green onion, chopped
- 1/4 cup parsley
- Pepper
- Salt

Directions:

1. Add all ingredients into the blender container. Secure the lid.
2. Start the blending at low speed, then quickly increase to highest speed and blend for 1 minute or until getting chunky consistency.
3. Serve and enjoy.

Nutritional Value (Amount per Serving):

- Calories 150
- Fat 6.4 g
- Carbohydrates 19.2 g
- Sugar 0.8 g
- Protein 6.4 g
- Cholesterol 0 mg

Delicious Tahini Dressing

Preparation Time: 10 minutes
Cooking Time: 1 minute
Serve: 8

Ingredients:

- 1/2 cup tahini
- 1 garlic clove
- 1 tsp onion powder
- 1 tsp vinegar
- 1 tsp Dijon mustard
- 1 tbsp fresh dill
- 1 tbsp fresh chives
- 3 tbsp lemon juice
- 1/2 cup water
- Salt

Directions:

1. Add all ingredients into the blender container. Secure the lid.
2. Start the blending at low speed, then quickly increase to highest speed and blend for 1 minute or until smooth.
3. Serve and enjoy.

Nutritional Value (Amount per Serving):

- Calories 94
- Fat 8.2 g
- Carbohydrates 4 g
- Sugar 0.3 g
- Protein 2.8 g
- Cholesterol 0 mg

Mango Mustard Sauce

Preparation Time: 10 minutes
Cooking Time: 1 minute
Serve: 4

Ingredients:

- 1/2 cup mango, chopped
- 1 tbsp fresh lemon juice
- 1 tsp red chili flakes
- 2 1/2 tbsp Dijon mustard
- 1/4 cup mayonnaise
- Salt

Directions:

1. Add all ingredients into the blender container. Secure the lid.
2. Start the blending at low speed, then quickly increase to highest speed and blend for 1 minute or until smooth.
3. Serve and enjoy.

Nutritional Value (Amount per Serving):

- Calories 77
- Fat 5.4 g
- Carbohydrates 7.2 g
- Sugar 3.9 g
- Protein 0.8 g
- Cholesterol 4 mg

Easy Hollandaise Sauce

Preparation Time: 10 minutes
Cooking Time: 1 minute
Serve: 12

Ingredients:

- 3 egg yolks
- 1/2 cup butter, melted
- 1 tbsp vinegar
- 3/4 tsp dry mustard
- Pepper
- Salt

Directions:

1. Add all ingredients into the blender container. Secure the lid.
2. Start the blending at low speed, then quickly increase to highest speed and blend for 1 minute or until thick & fluffy.
3. Serve and enjoy.

Nutritional Value (Amount per Serving):

- Calories 83
- Fat 8.9 g
- Carbohydrates 0.3 g
- Sugar 0.1 g
- Protein 0.8 g
- Cholesterol 73 mg

Italian Salad Dressing

Preparation Time: 10 minutes
Cooking Time: 1 minute
Serve: 8

Ingredients:

- 1/4 cup parmesan cheese, grated
- 1 1/2 tsp honey
- 1/2 tsp dried thyme
- 1/2 tsp dried parsley
- 1/2 tsp dried oregano
- 1 tsp dried basil
- 1 garlic clove
- 1/2 cup mayonnaise
- 1/3 cup olive oil
- 2 tbsp lime juice
- 1/4 cup vinegar
- Pepper
- Salt

Directions:

1. Add all ingredients into the blender container. Secure the lid.
2. Start the blending at low speed, then quickly increase to highest speed and blend for 1 minute or until smooth.
3. Serve and enjoy.

Nutritional Value (Amount per Serving):

- Calories 142
- Fat 13.5 g
- Carbohydrates 5.9 g
- Sugar 2.2 g
- Protein 0.5 g
- Cholesterol 4 mg

Easy Strawberry Dressing

Preparation Time: 10 minutes
Cooking Time: 1 minute
Serve: 4

Ingredients:

- 1 cup fresh strawberries
- 3/4 tbsp honey
- 1 tbsp vinegar
- 3 tbsp olive oil
- Pepper
- Salt

Directions:

1. Add all ingredients into the blender container. Secure the lid.
2. Start the blending at low speed, then quickly increase to highest speed and blend for 1 minute or until smooth.
3. Serve and enjoy.

Nutritional Value (Amount per Serving):

- Calories 114
- Fat 10.6 g
- Carbohydrates 6.1 g
- Sugar 5 g
- Protein 0.3 g
- Cholesterol 0 mg

Honey Mustard Dressing

Preparation Time: 10 minutes
Cooking Time: 1 minute
Serve: 8

Ingredients:

- 3/4 cup olive oil
- 1/3 cup vinegar
- 2 tbsp lime juice
- 1 garlic clove
- 1/4 cup Dijon mustard
- 1/4 cup honey
- Salt

Directions:

1. Add all ingredients into the blender container. Secure the lid.
2. Start the blending at low speed, then quickly increase to highest speed and blend for 1 minute or until smooth.
3. Serve and enjoy.

Nutritional Value (Amount per Serving):

- Calories 205
- Fat 19.2 g
- Carbohydrates 10.3 g
- Sugar 9 g
- Protein 0.4 g
- Cholesterol 0 mg

Classic Caesar Dressing

Preparation Time: 10 minutes
Cooking Time: 1 minute
Serve: 4

Ingredients:

- 1/2 cup olive oil
- 1 tsp Dijon mustard
- 2 tbsp fresh lime juice
- 1/3 cup parmesan cheese, grated
- 2 egg yolks
- 1 garlic clove
- 4 anchovy fillets, drained
- Pepper
- Salt

Directions:

1. Add all ingredients into the blender container. Secure the lid.
2. Start the blending at low speed, then quickly increase to highest speed and blend for 1 minute or until smooth.
3. Serve and enjoy.

Nutritional Value (Amount per Serving):

- Calories 266
- Fat 28.4 g
- Carbohydrates 2.6 g
- Sugar 0.4 g
- Protein 3.5 g
- Cholesterol 110 mg

Flavorful Peanut Sauce

Preparation Time: 10 minutes
Cooking Time: 1 minute
Serve: 8

Ingredients:

- 1/2 cup creamy peanut butter
- 3 tbsp water
- 1 tsp sriracha sauce
- 1/2 lemon juice
- 1 tbsp soy sauce
- 2 garlic cloves
- 1/2 tbsp fresh ginger, chopped

Directions:

1. Add all ingredients into the blender container. Secure the lid.
2. Start the blending at low speed, then quickly increase to highest speed and blend for 1 minute or until smooth.
3. Serve and enjoy.

Nutritional Value (Amount per Serving):

- Calories 99
- Fat 8.2 g
- Carbohydrates 3.9 g
- Sugar 1.6 g
- Protein 4.3 g
- Cholesterol 0 mg

Cheese Pepper Spread

Preparation Time: 10 minutes
Cooking Time: 1 minute
Serve: 20

Ingredients:

- 1 cup can roasted red peppers, drained
- 1/4 tsp red chili flakes
- 1 tsp lime juice
- 8 oz cream cheese
- 1 garlic clove
- 1/2 tsp dried basil
- Pepper
- Salt

Directions:

1. Add all ingredients into the blender container. Secure the lid.
2. Start the blending at low speed, then quickly increase to highest speed and blend for 1 minute or until smooth & creamy.
3. Serve and enjoy.

Nutritional Value (Amount per Serving):

- Calories 45
- Fat 4.1 g
- Carbohydrates 1.4 g
- Sugar 0.6 g
- Protein 1 g
- Cholesterol 12 mg

Mango Lemon Dressing

Preparation Time: 10 minutes
Cooking Time: 1 minute
Serve: 6

Ingredients:

- 1 cup mango, diced
- 1/2 tsp garlic powder
- 1/2 tsp ground cumin
- 1/4 cup cilantro
- 1 tbsp olive oil
- 1 tbsp vinegar
- 1 lemon juice
- Salt

Directions:

1. Add all ingredients into the blender container. Secure the lid.
2. Start the blending at low speed, then quickly increase to highest speed and blend for 1 minute or until smooth.
3. Serve and enjoy.

Nutritional Value (Amount per Serving):

- Calories 41
- Fat 2.5 g
- Carbohydrates 4.6 g
- Sugar 4 g
- Protein 0.4 g
- Cholesterol 0 mg

Creamy Tomatillo Dressing

Preparation Time: 10 minutes
Cooking Time: 1 minute
Serve: 16

Ingredients:

- 2 tomatillo, husked & chopped
- 1 jalapeno pepper, diced
- 1 lemon juice
- 1 garlic clove
- 1/2 cup cilantro
- 1 cup mayonnaise
- 1 cup buttermilk
- 1 packet ranch seasoning mix

Directions:

1. Add all ingredients into the blender container. Secure the lid.
2. Start the blending at low speed, then quickly increase to highest speed and blend for 1 minute or until smooth.
3. Serve and enjoy.

Nutritional Value (Amount per Serving):

- Calories 66
- Fat 5.1 g
- Carbohydrates 4.7 g
- Sugar 1.8 g
- Protein 0.7 g
- Cholesterol 4 mg

Salsa Dressing

Preparation Time: 10 minutes
Cooking Time: 1 minute
Serve: 6

Ingredients:

- 1 cup salsa
- 1/4 cup water
- 1/2 lemon juice
- 1 tsp ground cumin
- 1 avocado, scoop out the flesh
- 1/2 cup olive oil
- Pepper
- Salt

Directions:

1. Add all ingredients into the blender container. Secure the lid.
2. Start the blending at low speed, then quickly increase to highest speed and blend for 1 minute or until smooth.
3. Serve and enjoy.

Nutritional Value (Amount per Serving):

- Calories 226
- Fat 23.5 g
- Carbohydrates 5.8 g
- Sugar 1.6 g
- Protein 1.4 g
- Cholesterol 0 mg

Avocado Sandwich Spread

Preparation Time: 10 minutes
Cooking Time: 1 minute
Serve: 2

Ingredients:

- 1 avocado, scoop out the flesh
- 1 lime juice
- 2 tbsp green onion
- 1/4 cup cilantro
- 1/4 tsp paprika
- 14.5 oz can chickpeas, drained
- Pepper
- Salt

Directions:

1. Add all ingredients into the blender container. Secure the lid.
2. Start the blending at low speed, then quickly increase to highest speed and blend for 1 minute or until getting a chunky consistency.
3. Serve and enjoy.

Nutritional Value (Amount per Serving):

- Calories 458
- Fat 22 g
- Carbohydrates 57.6 g
- Sugar 1.1 g
- Protein 12.4 g
- Cholesterol 0 mg

Chapter 5: Desserts

Fluffy Strawberry Mousse

Preparation Time: 5 minutes
Cooking Time: 1 minute
Serve: 10

Ingredients:

- 1 cup strawberries
- 3 oz strawberry jello
- 1 cup hot water
- 3 tbsp sugar
- 5 tbsp mascarpone cheese
- 2 cups heavy whipping cream

Directions:

1. Add all ingredients into the blender container. Secure the lid.
2. Start the blending at low speed, then slowly increase to highest speed and blend for 1 minute or until smooth.
3. Pour into the container and place in the refrigerator for 6 hours.
4. Serve and enjoy.

Nutritional Value (Amount per Serving):

- Calories 120
- Fat 9.9 g
- Carbohydrates 6.8 g
- Sugar 5.5 g
- Protein 1.6 g
- Cholesterol 37 mg

Chocolate Mousse

Preparation Time: 5 minutes
Cooking Time: 1 minute
Serve: 4

Ingredients:

- 6 oz chocolate, melted
- 1/2 tsp vanilla
- 3 avocados, scoop out the flesh
- 1/2 cup cocoa powder
- 3 tbsp coconut oil, melted

Directions:

1. Add all ingredients into the blender container. Secure the lid.
2. Start the blending at low speed, then slowly increase to highest speed and blend for 1 minute or until smooth.
3. Pour into the container and place in the refrigerator for 1 hour.
4. Serve and enjoy.

Nutritional Value (Amount per Serving):

- Calories 648
- Fat 53.6 g
- Carbohydrates 44.2 g
- Sugar 22.9 g
- Protein 8.1 g
- Cholesterol 10 mg

Raspberry Mousse

Preparation Time: 5 minutes
Cooking Time: 1 minute
Serve: 2

Ingredients:

- 1 cup frozen raspberries
- 1 tbsp almond milk
- 1 frozen banana
- 1 avocado, scoop out the flesh

Directions:

1. Add all ingredients into the blender container. Secure the lid.
2. Start the blending at low speed, then slowly increase to highest speed and blend for 1 minute or until smooth.
3. Pour into the container and place in the refrigerator for 1 hour.
4. Serve and enjoy.

Nutritional Value (Amount per Serving):

- Calories 351
- Fat 21.6 g
- Carbohydrates 41.8 g
- Sugar 28 g
- Protein 3 g
- Cholesterol 0 mg

Easy Lemon Curd

Preparation Time: 5 minutes
Cooking Time: 5 minutes
Serve: 4

Ingredients:

- 5 eggs
- 1/2 cup butter, cut into chunks
- 1 1/2 cups sugar
- 1/2 cup lemon juice
- 1/8 tsp salt

Directions:

1. Add all ingredients into the blender container. Secure the lid.
2. Start the blending at low speed, then slowly increase to the highest speed and blend for 5 minutes.
3. Pour into the container and place in the refrigerator for 2 hours.
4. Serve and enjoy.

Nutritional Value (Amount per Serving):

- Calories 571
- Fat 28.7 g
- Carbohydrates 76.1 g
- Sugar 76.1 g
- Protein 7.4 g
- Cholesterol 266 mg

Mango Sorbet

Preparation Time: 5 minutes
Cooking Time: 1 minute
Serve: 5

Ingredients:

- 4 cups mangoes, diced
- 3 cups ice cubes
- 1 cup sugar
- 1 tsp lime juice

Directions:

1. Add all ingredients into the blender container. Secure the lid.
2. Start the blending at low speed, then slowly increase to the highest speed and blend for 5 minutes or until smooth.
3. Serve and enjoy.

Nutritional Value (Amount per Serving):

- Calories 229
- Fat 0.5 g
- Carbohydrates 60.5 g
- Sugar 58.2 g
- Protein 1.1 g
- Cholesterol 0 mg

Cherry Yogurt

Preparation Time: 5 minutes
Cooking Time: 5 minutes
Serve: 6

Ingredients:

- 16 oz frozen cherries
- 2 tbsp lime juice
- 1 cup plain yogurt
- 1/2 cup maple syrup
- Pinch of salt

Directions:

1. Add all ingredients into the blender container. Secure the lid.
2. Start the blending at low speed, then slowly increase to the highest speed and blend for 5 minutes or until smooth.
3. Pour into the container and place in the refrigerator for 1 hour.
4. Serve and enjoy.

Nutritional Value (Amount per Serving):

- Calories 136
- Fat 0.9 g
- Carbohydrates 30 g
- Sugar 25.6 g
- Protein 3.1 g
- Cholesterol 2 mg

Raspberry Sorbet

Preparation Time: 5 minutes
Cooking Time: 1 minute
Serve: 2

Ingredients:

- 1/2 cup frozen cherries, pitted
- 1 1/3 cups frozen raspberries
- 1 frozen banana
- 2/3 cup almond milk

Directions:

1. Add all ingredients into the blender container. Secure the lid.
2. Start the blending at low speed, then slowly increase to highest speed and blend for 1 minute or until smooth.
3. Serve and enjoy.

Nutritional Value (Amount per Serving):

- Calories 429
- Fat 20.5 g
- Carbohydrates 62.3 g
- Sugar 49.9 g
- Protein 4.9 g
- Cholesterol 5 mg

Easy Strawberry Ice Cream

Preparation Time: 5 minutes
Cooking Time: 1 minute
Serve: 1

Ingredients:

- 10 frozen strawberries
- 1/2 tsp vanilla
- 1 scoop vanilla protein powder
- 1/2 frozen banana
- 1/4 cup full-fat coconut milk

Directions:

1. Add all ingredients into the blender container. Secure the lid.
2. Start the blending at low speed, then slowly increase to highest speed and blend for 1 minute or until smooth.
3. Serve and enjoy.

Nutritional Value (Amount per Serving):

- Calories 688
- Fat 4.3 g
- Carbohydrates 142.6 g
- Sugar 98 g
- Protein 24.8 g
- Cholesterol 15 mg

Strawberry Cheesecake Ice Cream

Preparation Time: 5 minutes
Cooking Time: 1 minute
Serve: 2

Ingredients:

- 1 cup frozen strawberries
- 6 drops liquid stevia
- 1 tbsp cream cheese
- 1/4 cup greek yogurt
- 3/4 cup almond milk

Directions:

1. Add all ingredients into the blender container. Secure the lid.
2. Start the blending at low speed, then slowly increase to highest speed and blend for 1 minute or until smooth.
3. Serve and enjoy.

Nutritional Value (Amount per Serving):

- Calories 268
- Fat 23.7 g
- Carbohydrates 12.6 g
- Sugar 8.5 g
- Protein 5 g
- Cholesterol 7 mg

Strawberry Banana Sorbet

Preparation Time: 5 minutes
Cooking Time: 1 minute
Serve: 6

Ingredients:

- 1/2 lb frozen strawberry
- 1/2 lb frozen banana
- 1/3 cup honey
- 3 tbsp fresh lemon juice

Directions:

1. Add all ingredients into the blender container. Secure the lid.
2. Start the blending at low speed, then slowly increase to highest speed and blend for 1 minute or until smooth.
3. Pour into the container and place in the refrigerator for 3 hours.
4. Serve and enjoy.

Nutritional Value (Amount per Serving):

- Calories 106
- Fat 0.7 g
- Carbohydrates 25.2 g
- Sugar 21.9 g
- Protein 1.2 g
- Cholesterol 3 mg

Blueberry Ice Cream

Preparation Time: 5 minutes
Cooking Time: 1 minute
Serve: 4

Ingredients:

- 1 cup heavy whipping cream
- 1 1/2 cups frozen blueberries
- 4 tbsp erythritol

Directions:

1. Add all ingredients into the blender container. Secure the lid.
2. Start the blending at low speed, then slowly increase to highest speed and blend for 1 minute or until smooth.
3. Pour into the container and place in the refrigerator for 4 hours.
4. Serve and enjoy.

Nutritional Value (Amount per Serving):

- Calories 135
- Fat 11.3 g
- Carbohydrates 23.7 g
- Sugar 20.4 g
- Protein 1 g
- Cholesterol 41 mg

Coconut Cherry Popsicles

Preparation Time: 5 minutes
Cooking Time: 1 minute
Serve: 10

Ingredients:

- 14 oz can full-fat coconut milk
- 1 tsp maple syrup
- 2 cups fresh cherries, pitted

Directions:

1. Add all ingredients into the blender container. Secure the lid.
2. Start the blending at low speed, then slowly increase to highest speed and blend for 1 minute or until smooth.
3. Pour into the popsicle molds and place in refrigerator until set.
4. Serve and enjoy.

Nutritional Value (Amount per Serving):

- Calories 92
- Fat 7.3 g
- Carbohydrates 5.8 g
- Sugar 1 g
- Protein 0.7 g
- Cholesterol 0 mg

Peanut Butter Mousse

Preparation Time: 5 minutes
Cooking Time: 5 minutes
Serve: 2

Ingredients:

- 3 tbsp smooth peanut butter
- 1/2 cup chocolate chips
- 1/4 cup sugar
- 14 oz firm tofu, drained & cubed
- 1/2 cup almond milk

Directions:

1. Heat almond milk in a pan until just warm.
2. Add all ingredients into the blender container. Secure the lid.
3. Start the blending at low speed, then slowly increase to highest speed and blend for 1 minute or until smooth.
4. Pour into the container and place in the refrigerator for 4 hours.
5. Serve and enjoy.

Nutritional Value (Amount per Serving):

- Calories 646
- Fat 35.8 g
- Carbohydrates 63 g
- Sugar 54.5 g
- Protein 26.5 g
- Cholesterol 12 mg

Nutella Banana Ice Cream

Preparation Time: 5 minutes
Cooking Time: 1 minute
Serve: 4

Ingredients:

- 4 frozen banana
- 1/2 cup Nutella

Directions:

1. Add all ingredients into the blender container. Secure the lid.
2. Start the blending at low speed, then slowly increase to highest speed and blend for 1 minute or until smooth.
3. Pour into the container and place in the refrigerator for 2 hours.
4. Serve and enjoy.

Nutritional Value (Amount per Serving):

- Calories 135
- Fat 3.4 g
- Carbohydrates 22.9 g
- Sugar 17.5 g
- Protein 3.3 g
- Cholesterol 10 mg

Yummy Blueberry Yogurt

Preparation Time: 5 minutes
Cooking Time: 1 minute
Serve: 2

Ingredients:

- 1 cup frozen blueberries
- 1 tsp vanilla
- 2 tbsp maple syrup
- 1 1/2 cups almond milk yogurt
- Pinch of salt

Directions:

1. Add all ingredients into the blender container. Secure the lid.
2. Start the blending at low speed, then slowly increase to highest speed and blend for 1 minute or until smooth.
3. Serve and enjoy.

Nutritional Value (Amount per Serving):

- Calories 212
- Fat 4.8 g
- Carbohydrates 42.2 g
- Sugar 32.9 g
- Protein 2.8 g
- Cholesterol 0 mg

Coconut Popsicles

Preparation Time: 5 minutes
Cooking Time: 1 minute
Serve: 4

Ingredients:

- 14 oz coconut milk
- 1 banana
- 1 tbsp maple syrup

Directions:

1. Add all ingredients into the blender container. Secure the lid.
2. Start the blending at low speed, then slowly increase to highest speed and blend for 1 minute or until smooth.
3. Pour into the popsicle molds and place in refrigerator until set.
4. Serve and enjoy.

Nutritional Value (Amount per Serving):

- Calories 268
- Fat 23.8 g
- Carbohydrates 15.6 g
- Sugar 9.9 g
- Protein 2.6 g
- Cholesterol 0 mg

Peach Ice Cream

Preparation Time: 5 minutes
Cooking Time: 1 minute
Serve: 4

Ingredients:

- 3 cups frozen peach slices
- 2 tbsp honey
- 1 1/2 cups almond milk

Directions:

1. Add all ingredients into the blender container. Secure the lid.
2. Start the blending at low speed, then slowly increase to highest speed and blend for 1 minute or until smooth.
3. Pour into the container and place in the refrigerator for 4 hours.
4. Serve and enjoy.

Nutritional Value (Amount per Serving):

- Calories 415
- Fat 21.7 g
- Carbohydrates 58.6 g
- Sugar 53.2 g
- Protein 3.3 g
- Cholesterol 0 mg

Easy Cherry Sorbet

Preparation Time: 5 minutes
Cooking Time: 1 minute
Serve: 6

Ingredients:

- 1 lb frozen cherries, pitted
- 1 tsp fresh lemon juice
- 1 cup sugar

Directions:

1. Add all ingredients into the blender container. Secure the lid.
2. Start the blending at low speed, then slowly increase to highest speed and blend for 1 minute or until smooth.
3. Pour into the container and place in the refrigerator for 5 hours.
4. Serve and enjoy.

Nutritional Value (Amount per Serving):

- Calories 160
- Fat 0.3 g
- Carbohydrates 41.7 g
- Sugar 40.2 g
- Protein 0.7 g
- Cholesterol 0 mg

Pineapple Mango Sorbet

Preparation Time: 5 minutes
Cooking Time: 1 minute
Serve: 4

Ingredients:

- 2 cups frozen pineapple
- 2 cups frozen mango
- 1 tbsp maple syrup

Directions:

1. Add all ingredients into the blender container. Secure the lid.
2. Start the blending at low speed, then slowly increase to highest speed and blend for 1 minute or until smooth.
3. Serve and enjoy.

Nutritional Value (Amount per Serving):

- Calories 178
- Fat 2.6 g
- Carbohydrates 37.3 g
- Sugar 32.7 g
- Protein 2.5 g
- Cholesterol 10 mg

Easy Pumpkin Mousse

Preparation Time: 5 minutes
Cooking Time: 1 minute
Serve: 4

Ingredients:

- 1/2 cup pumpkin puree
- 1 tsp vanilla
- 1 tbsp pumpkin pie spice
- 1/4 cup maple syrup
- 1 cup coconut cream
- Pinch of salt

Directions:

1. Add all ingredients into the blender container. Secure the lid.
2. Start the blending at low speed, then slowly increase to highest speed and blend for 1 minute or until smooth.
3. Pour into the container and place in the refrigerator for 2 hours.
4. Serve and enjoy.

Nutritional Value (Amount per Serving):

- Calories 208
- Fat 14.6 g
- Carbohydrates 20.1 g
- Sugar 15 g
- Protein 1.8 g
- Cholesterol 0 mg

Perfect Pineapple Ice Cream

Preparation Time: 5 minutes
Cooking Time: 5 minutes
Serve: 6

Ingredients:

- 20 oz can crushed pineapple
- 1/2 cup heavy cream
- 1 1/2 cups pineapple juice

Directions:

1. Add all ingredients into the blender container. Secure the lid.
2. Start the blending at low speed, then slowly increase to the highest speed and blend for 5 minutes or until smooth.
3. Pour into the container and place in the refrigerator for 4 hours.
4. Serve and enjoy.

Nutritional Value (Amount per Serving):

- Calories 118
- Fat 3.8 g
- Carbohydrates 20.9 g
- Sugar 15.7 g
- Protein 0.8 g
- Cholesterol 14 mg

Blueberry Sorbet

Preparation Time: 5 minutes
Cooking Time: 1 minute
Serve: 4

Ingredients:

- 4 cups frozen blueberries
- 1/2 cup water
- 2 tbsp honey

Directions:

1. Add all ingredients into the blender container. Secure the lid.
2. Start the blending at low speed, then slowly increase to highest speed and blend for 1 minute or until smooth.
3. Pour into the container and place in the refrigerator for 4 hours.
4. Serve and enjoy.

Nutritional Value (Amount per Serving):

- Calories 115
- Fat 0.5 g
- Carbohydrates 29.7 g
- Sugar 23 g
- Protein 1.1 g
- Cholesterol 0 mg

Orange Pineapple Sorbet

Preparation Time: 5 minutes
Cooking Time: 1 minute
Serve: 4

Ingredients:

- 1/2 orange zest
- 3 cups frozen pineapple chunks

Directions:

1. Add all ingredients into the blender container. Secure the lid.
2. Start the blending at low speed, then slowly increase to highest speed and blend for 1 minute or until smooth.
3. Pour into the container and place in the refrigerator for 4 hours.
4. Serve and enjoy.

Nutritional Value (Amount per Serving):

- Calories 159
- Fat 0.2 g
- Carbohydrates 41 g
- Sugar 38.8 g
- Protein 0.8 g
- Cholesterol 0 mg

Pumpkin Mousse

Preparation Time: 5 minutes
Cooking Time: 1 minute
Serve: 10

Ingredients:

- 15 oz can pumpkin puree
- 3/4 cup heavy cream
- 2 tbsp pumpkin spice
- 2 tsp vanilla
- 1/2 cup Swerve
- 12 oz cream cheese, softened

Directions:

1. Add all ingredients into the blender container. Secure the lid.
2. Start the blending at low speed, then slowly increase to highest speed and blend for 1 minute or until smooth.
3. Pour into the container and place in the refrigerator for 2 hours.
4. Serve and enjoy.

Nutritional Value (Amount per Serving):

- Calories 219
- Fat 15.3 g
- Carbohydrates 17.1 g
- Sugar 6.3 g
- Protein 4.3 g
- Cholesterol 50 mg

Chia Chocolate Pudding

Preparation Time: 5 minutes
Cooking Time: 1 minute
Serve: 4

Ingredients:

- 6 tbsp chia seeds
- 1 tsp vanilla
- 2 tbsp cocoa powder
- 1/4 cup honey
- 1 cup almond milk
- Pinch of salt

Directions:

1. Add all ingredients into the blender container. Secure the lid.
2. Start the blending at low speed, then slowly increase to highest speed and blend for 1 minute or until smooth.
3. Pour into the container and place in the refrigerator for 3 hours.
4. Serve and enjoy.

Nutritional Value (Amount per Serving):

- Calories 418
- Fat 27.7 g
- Carbohydrates 40.3 g
- Sugar 19.6 g
- Protein 8.9 g
- Cholesterol 0 mg

Chapter 6: Drinks

Healthy Avocado Spinach Smoothie

Preparation Time: 5 minutes
Cooking Time: 1 minute
Serve: 2

Ingredients:

- 2 cups spinach
- 3/4 cup almond milk
- 1 tbsp almond butter
- 1/2 avocado, scoop out the flesh
- 1 banana

Directions:

1. Add all ingredients into the blender container. Secure the lid.
2. Start the blending on low speed, then quickly increase to highest speed and blend for 1 minute or until smooth.
3. Serve and enjoy.

Nutritional Value (Amount per Serving):

- Calories 418
- Fat 36.1 g
- Carbohydrates 25.4 g
- Sugar 11 g
- Protein 6.2 g
- Cholesterol 0 mg

Cinnamon Apple Smoothie

Preparation Time: 5 minutes
Cooking Time: 1 minute
Serve: 2

Ingredients:

- 2 apples, sliced
- 1 cup ice cubes
- 3/4 tsp ground cinnamon
- 1/2 tsp vanilla
- 1 1/2 tbsp chia seeds
- 2 tbsp almond butter
- 1/3 cup rolled oats
- 1 1/2 cups almond milk

Directions:

1. Add all ingredients into the blender container. Secure the lid.
2. Start the blending on low speed, then quickly increase to highest speed and blend for 1 minute or until smooth.
3. Serve and enjoy.

Nutritional Value (Amount per Serving):

- Calories 685
- Fat 53 g
- Carbohydrates 53 g
- Sugar 30 g
- Protein 9 g
- Cholesterol 0 mg

Banana Peanut Butter Smoothie

Preparation Time: 5 minutes
Cooking Time: 1 minute
Serve: 2

Ingredients:

- 1 1/2 cups almond milk
- 1 cup ice
- 1 tbsp cocoa powder
- 1/2 tsp vanilla
- 2 tbsp Greek yogurt
- 2 tbsp peanut butter
- 2 bananas

Directions:

1. Add all ingredients into the blender container. Secure the lid.
2. Start the blending on low speed, then quickly increase to highest speed and blend for 1 minute or until smooth.
3. Serve and enjoy.

Nutritional Value (Amount per Serving):

- Calories 622
- Fat 51 g
- Carbohydrates 41 g
- Sugar 22 g
- Protein 9 g
- Cholesterol 0 mg

Healthy Raspberry Smoothie

Preparation Time: 5 minutes
Cooking Time: 1 minute
Serve: 2

Ingredients:

- 2 cups raspberries
- 1 cup yogurt
- 1 cup almond milk
- 1 lime juice
- 1 lime zest
- 1 tbsp honey

Directions:

1. Add all ingredients into the blender container. Secure the lid.
2. Start the blending on low speed, then quickly increase to highest speed and blend for 1 minute or until smooth.
3. Serve and enjoy.

Nutritional Value (Amount per Serving):

- Calories 459
- Fat 30.9 g
- Carbohydrates 38.6 g
- Sugar 26.7 g
- Protein 11.2 g
- Cholesterol 7 mg

Banana Coffee Smoothie

Preparation Time: 5 minutes
Cooking Time: 1 minute
Serve: 2

Ingredients:

- 1 cup brewed coffee
- 1 tbsp cocoa powder
- 1 cup milk
- 1 tbsp almond butter
- 1 banana

Directions:

1. Add all ingredients into the blender container. Secure the lid.
2. Start the blending on low speed, then quickly increase to highest speed and blend for 1 minute or until smooth.
3. Serve and enjoy.

Nutritional Value (Amount per Serving):

- Calories 170
- Fat 7.6 g
- Carbohydrates 22.5 g
- Sugar 13.1 g
- Protein 7 g
- Cholesterol 10 mg

Healthy Berry Smoothie

Preparation Time: 5 minutes
Cooking Time: 1 minute
Serve: 2

Ingredients:

- 1/2 cup blueberries
- 1 cup strawberries
- 1 tbsp honey
- 1 cup almond milk
- 1 tbsp chia seeds
- 1/3 cup oats

Directions:

1. Add all ingredients into the blender container. Secure the lid.
2. Start the blending on low speed, then quickly increase to highest speed and blend for 1 minute or until smooth.
3. Serve and enjoy.

Nutritional Value (Amount per Serving):

- Calories 403
- Fat 29.9 g
- Carbohydrates 35.3 g
- Sugar 19.9 g
- Protein 5.3 g
- Cholesterol 0 mg

Watermelon Strawberry Smoothie

Preparation Time: 5 minutes
Cooking Time: 1 minute
Serve: 2

Ingredients:

- 1 tbsp hemp seeds
- 3/4 cup yogurt
- 1 cup strawberries
- 4 cups watermelon

Directions:

1. Add all ingredients into the blender container. Secure the lid.
2. Start the blending on low speed, then quickly increase to highest speed and blend for 1 minute or until smooth.
3. Serve and enjoy.

Nutritional Value (Amount per Serving):

- Calories 180
- Fat 1.7 g
- Carbohydrates 34.8 g
- Sugar 28.7 g
- Protein 7.5 g
- Cholesterol 6 mg

Mix Berry Smoothie

Preparation Time: 5 minutes
Cooking Time: 1 minute
Serve: 2

Ingredients:

- 1 banana
- 1/2 cup blueberries
- 1/2 cup raspberries
- 1 cup strawberries
- 1 cup almond milk
- 1/4 tsp vanilla

Directions:

1. Add all ingredients into the blender container. Secure the lid.
2. Start the blending on low speed, then quickly increase to highest speed and blend for 1 minute or until smooth.
3. Serve and enjoy.

Nutritional Value (Amount per Serving):

- Calories 390
- Fat 29.4 g
- Carbohydrates 34.7 g
- Sugar 19.8 g
- Protein 4.5 g
- Cholesterol 0 mg

Green Pineapple Smoothie

Preparation Time: 5 minutes
Cooking Time: 1 minute
Serve: 2

Ingredients:

- 1/2 cup pineapple
- 1 banana
- 1/2 cup mango
- 2 cups spinach
- 1 cup almond milk
- 1 cup Greek yogurt

Directions:

1. Add all ingredients into the blender container. Secure the lid.
2. Start the blending on low speed, then quickly increase to highest speed and blend for 1 minute or until smooth.
3. Serve and enjoy.

Nutritional Value (Amount per Serving):

- Calories 381
- Fat 29.1 g
- Carbohydrates 32.8 g
- Sugar 21.1 g
- Protein 4.8 g
- Cholesterol 0 mg

Spinach Cherry Banana Smoothie

Preparation Time: 5 minutes
Cooking Time: 1 minute
Serve: 2

Ingredients:

- 1 cup spinach
- 1 cup frozen cherries
- 1 banana
- 1/2 cup ice
- 1 cup almond milk

Directions:

1. Add all ingredients into the blender container. Secure the lid.
2. Start the blending on low speed, then quickly increase to highest speed and blend for 1 minute or until smooth.
3. Serve and enjoy.

Nutritional Value (Amount per Serving):

- Calories 368
- Fat 29 g
- Carbohydrates 29 g
- Sugar 18 g
- Protein 4 g
- Cholesterol 0 mg

Peach Raspberry Smoothie

Preparation Time: 5 minutes
Cooking Time: 1 minute
Serve: 1

Ingredients:

- 3/4 cup peach, chopped
- 1 cup raspberries
- 1 tsp honey
- 1/3 cup almond milk
- 1/4 cup Greek yogurt

Directions:

1. Add all ingredients into the blender container. Secure the lid.
2. Start the blending on low speed, then quickly increase to highest speed and blend for 1 minute or until smooth.
3. Serve and enjoy.

Nutritional Value (Amount per Serving):

- Calories 313
- Fat 20 g
- Carbohydrates 35 g
- Sugar 24 g
- Protein 4 g
- Cholesterol 0 mg

Creamy Strawberry Milkshake

Preparation Time: 5 minutes
Cooking Time: 1 minute
Serve: 2

Ingredients:

- 1/2 lb strawberries
- 1/2 cup milk
- 1 tsp vanilla
- 2 cups vanilla ice cream
- 1 1/2 tbsp sugar

Directions:

1. Add all ingredients into the blender container. Secure the lid.
2. Start the blending on low speed, then quickly increase to highest speed and blend for 1 minute or until smooth.
3. Serve and enjoy.

Nutritional Value (Amount per Serving):

- Calories 244
- Fat 8.6 g
- Carbohydrates 37 g
- Sugar 31 g
- Protein 5 g
- Cholesterol 34 mg

Easy Pineapple Lemonade

Preparation Time: 5 minutes
Cooking Time: 1 minute
Serve: 2

Ingredients:

- 2 cups pineapple chunks
- 1 cup ice cubes
- 1 lemon juice

Directions:

1. Add all ingredients into the blender container. Secure the lid.
2. Start the blending on low speed, then quickly increase to highest speed and blend for 1 minute or until smooth.
3. Serve and enjoy.

Nutritional Value (Amount per Serving):

- Calories 82
- Fat 0.2 g
- Carbohydrates 21.7 g
- Sugar 16.3 g
- Protein 0.9 g
- Cholesterol 0 mg

Cinnamon Banana Smoothie

Preparation Time: 5 minutes
Cooking Time: 1 minute
Serve: 2

Ingredients:

- 1 banana
- 1/2 cup ice
- 1/8 tsp cinnamon
- 1/3 tsp vanilla
- 1/4 cup walnuts
- 1/3 cup rolled oats
- 1 cup almond milk
- 1 apple, peel & dice
- Pinch of salt

Directions:

1. Add all ingredients into the blender container. Secure the lid.
2. Start the blending on low speed, then quickly increase to highest speed and blend for 1 minute or until smooth.
3. Serve and enjoy.

Nutritional Value (Amount per Serving):

- Calories 537
- Fat 39.1 g
- Carbohydrates 46 g
- Sugar 23 g
- Protein 9.3 g
- Cholesterol 0 mg

Healthy Tropical Smoothie

Preparation Time: 5 minutes
Cooking Time: 1 minute
Serve: 2

Ingredients:

- 1/2 cup pineapple
- 1/2 cup mango
- 1/2 banana
- 1 tbsp orange juice
- 1/2 cup coconut milk

Directions:

1. Add all ingredients into the blender container. Secure the lid.
2. Start the blending on low speed, then quickly increase to highest speed and blend for 1 minute or until smooth.
3. Serve and enjoy.

Nutritional Value (Amount per Serving):

- Calories 213
- Fat 14.6 g
- Carbohydrates 22.5 g
- Sugar 16 g
- Protein 2.3 g
- Cholesterol 0 mg

Healthy Orange Smoothie

Preparation Time: 5 minutes
Cooking Time: 1 minute
Serve: 1

Ingredients:

- 1 cup orange juice
- 1/2 cup carrots, chopped
- 1/2 tsp turmeric
- 1 tsp ginger, minced
- 1 banana

Directions:

1. Add all ingredients into the blender container. Secure the lid.
2. Start the blending on low speed, then quickly increase to highest speed and blend for 1 minute or until smooth.
3. Serve and enjoy.

Nutritional Value (Amount per Serving):

- Calories 250
- Fat 1.1 g
- Carbohydrates 60.1 g
- Sugar 38 g
- Protein 3.7 g
- Cholesterol 0 mg

Sweet Avocado Smoothie

Preparation Time: 5 minutes
Cooking Time: 1 minute
Serve: 2

Ingredients:

- 2 avocados, scoop out the flesh
- 1 cup ice
- 1 cup almond milk
- 1/3 cup condensed milk

Directions:

1. Add all ingredients into the blender container. Secure the lid.
2. Start the blending on low speed, then quickly increase to highest speed and blend for 1 minute or until smooth.
3. Serve and enjoy.

Nutritional Value (Amount per Serving):

- Calories 500
- Fat 38 g
- Carbohydrates 37 g
- Sugar 31 g
- Protein 7 g
- Cholesterol 17 mg

Creamy Cherry Smoothie

Preparation Time: 5 minutes
Cooking Time: 1 minute
Serve: 2

Ingredients:

- 1 1/2 cups cherries
- 1 cup Greek yogurt
- 1 banana
- 1 1/2 cups apple juice

Directions:

1. Add all ingredients into the blender container. Secure the lid.
2. Start the blending on low speed, then quickly increase to highest speed and blend for 1 minute or until smooth.
3. Serve and enjoy.

Nutritional Value (Amount per Serving):

- Calories 163
- Fat 0.6 g
- Carbohydrates 40 g
- Sugar 29 g
- Protein 1.3 g
- Cholesterol 0 mg

Spinach Cucumber Smoothie

Preparation Time: 5 minutes
Cooking Time: 1 minute
Serve: 4

Ingredients:

- 1 avocado, scoop out the flesh
- 1 cucumber
- 1 1/2 cups spinach
- 1 apple, diced
- 4 dates, pitted
- 2 cups almond milk

Directions:

1. Add all ingredients into the blender container. Secure the lid.
2. Start the blending on low speed, then quickly increase to highest speed and blend for 1 minute or until smooth.
3. Serve and enjoy.

Nutritional Value (Amount per Serving):

- Calories 445
- Fat 38 g
- Carbohydrates 28 g
- Sugar 16 g
- Protein 4.9 g
- Cholesterol 0 mg

Coffee Milkshake

Preparation Time: 5 minutes
Cooking Time: 1 minute
Serve: 2

Ingredients:

- 2 tbsp cocoa powder
- 2 tbsp instant coffee
- 3/4 cup milk
- 4 scoops vanilla ice cream

Directions:

1. Add all ingredients into the blender container. Secure the lid.
2. Start the blending on low speed, then quickly increase to highest speed and blend for 1 minute or until smooth.
3. Serve and enjoy.

Nutritional Value (Amount per Serving):

- Calories 332
- Fat 16 g
- Carbohydrates 39 g
- Sugar 32 g
- Protein 8 g
- Cholesterol 66 mg

Kiwi Strawberry Smoothie

Preparation Time: 5 minutes
Cooking Time: 1 minute
Serve: 2

Ingredients:

- 2 cups strawberries
- 1/2 tsp vanilla
- 1 cup almond milk
- 1 banana
- 2 kiwi, peeled & diced

Directions:

1. Add all ingredients into the blender container. Secure the lid.
2. Start the blending on low speed, then quickly increase to highest speed and blend for 1 minute or until smooth.
3. Serve and enjoy.

Nutritional Value (Amount per Serving):

- Calories 424
- Fat 29 g
- Carbohydrates 42 g
- Sugar 25 g
- Protein 5 g
- Cholesterol 0 mg

Watermelon Strawberry Smoothie

Preparation Time: 5 minutes
Cooking Time: 1 minute
Serve: 2

Ingredients:

- 3 1/2 cups watermelon
- 8 oz strawberries

Directions:

1. Add all ingredients into the blender container. Secure the lid.
2. Start the blending on low speed, then quickly increase to highest speed and blend for 1 minute or until smooth.
3. Serve and enjoy.

Nutritional Value (Amount per Serving):

- Calories 116
- Fat 0.7 g
- Carbohydrates 28.7 g
- Sugar 21 g
- Protein 2.3 g
- Cholesterol 0 mg

Easy Strawberry Protein Shake

Preparation Time: 5 minutes
Cooking Time: 1 minute
Serve: 2

Ingredients:

- 8 strawberries
- 5 drops liquid stevia
- 1 tsp vanilla
- 2 1/2 cups almond milk
- 2 scoops whey protein powder

Directions:

1. Add all ingredients into the blender container. Secure the lid.
2. Start the blending on low speed, then quickly increase to highest speed and blend for 1 minute or until smooth.
3. Serve and enjoy.

Nutritional Value (Amount per Serving):

- Calories 216
- Fat 5 g
- Carbohydrates 17 g
- Sugar 11 g
- Protein 23 g
- Cholesterol 65 mg

Mango Strawberry Smoothie

Preparation Time: 5 minutes
Cooking Time: 1 minute
Serve: 2

Ingredients:

- 1/2 cup strawberry
- 1/2 cup mango
- 1 tbsp honey
- 1 cup orange juice
- 3 tbsp water
- 3/4 cup orange juice

Directions:

1. Add all ingredients into the blender container. Secure the lid.
2. Start the blending on low speed, then quickly increase to highest speed and blend for 1 minute or until smooth.
3. Serve and enjoy.

Nutritional Value (Amount per Serving):

- Calories 166
- Fat 0.7 g
- Carbohydrates 40.2 g
- Sugar 34.2 g
- Protein 2.1 g
- Cholesterol 0 mg

Mango Pineapple Peach Smoothie

Preparation Time: 5 minutes
Cooking Time: 1 minute
Serve: 2

Ingredients:

- 1/2 cup mango
- 1/2 cup pineapple
- 1/2 cup peaches
- 2 tbsp protein powder
- 1/2 tbsp honey
- 1 tbsp ginger, grated
- 3/4 cup coconut milk
- 1/2 tbsp lemon zest
- 1 lemon juice

Directions:

1. Add all ingredients into the blender container. Secure the lid.
2. Start the blending on low speed, then quickly increase to highest speed and blend for 1 minute or until smooth.
3. Serve and enjoy.

Nutritional Value (Amount per Serving):

- Calories 293
- Fat 21 g
- Carbohydrates 26 g
- Sugar 20 g
- Protein 3 g
- Cholesterol 0 mg

Healthy Oatmeal Smoothie

Preparation Time: 5 minutes
Cooking Time: 1 minute
Serve: 2

Ingredients:

- 1/4 cup quick oats
- 1/2 tsp cinnamon
- 1/2 tsp vanilla
- 1/4 cup maple syrup
- 1 tbsp peanut butter
- 1/2 cup almond milk
- 1 banana
- Pinch of salt

Directions:

1. Add all ingredients into the blender container. Secure the lid.
2. Start the blending on low speed, then quickly increase to highest speed and blend for 1 minute or until smooth.
3. Serve and enjoy.

Nutritional Value (Amount per Serving):

- Calories 261
- Fat 5 g
- Carbohydrates 51 g
- Sugar 33 g
- Protein 4 g
- Cholesterol 51 mg

Thick & Creamy Banana Smoothie

Preparation Time: 5 minutes
Cooking Time: 1 minute
Serve: 2

Ingredients:

- 2 bananas
- 2 tbsp maple syrup
- 1/2 cup almond milk
- 1 cup Greek yogurt

Directions:

1. Add all ingredients into the blender container. Secure the lid.
2. Start the blending on low speed, then quickly increase to highest speed and blend for 1 minute or until smooth.
3. Serve and enjoy.

Nutritional Value (Amount per Serving):

- Calories 295
- Fat 14.7 g
- Carbohydrates 43.7 g
- Sugar 28.3 g
- Protein 2.7 g
- Cholesterol 0 mg

Banana Kiwi Smoothie

Preparation Time: 5 minutes
Cooking Time: 1 minute
Serve: 2

Ingredients:

- 1 banana
- 1 cup ice cubes
- 1 cup Greek yogurt
- 1 lime juice
- 1/2 cup almond milk
- 2 kiwi, peel & chopped

Directions:

1. Add all ingredients into the blender container. Secure the lid.
2. Start the blending on low speed, then quickly increase to highest speed and blend for 1 minute or until smooth.
3. Serve and enjoy.

Nutritional Value (Amount per Serving):

- Calories 237
- Fat 14.9 g
- Carbohydrates 27 g
- Sugar 16 g
- Protein 2.9 g
- Cholesterol 0 mg

Peach Lemonade

Preparation Time: 5 minutes
Cooking Time: 1 minute
Serve: 2

Ingredients:

- 2 cups peach slices
- 1 cup ice cubes
- 2 lemon juice
- 1/4 cup sugar

Directions:

1. Add all ingredients into the blender container. Secure the lid.
2. Start the blending on low speed, then quickly increase to highest speed and blend for 1 minute or until desired consistency.
3. Serve and enjoy.

Nutritional Value (Amount per Serving):

- Calories 153
- Fat 0.4 g
- Carbohydrates 39 g
- Sugar 39 g
- Protein 1.4 g
- Cholesterol 0 mg

Cookie Shake

Preparation Time: 5 minutes
Cooking Time: 1 minute
Serve: 1

Ingredients:

- 1 chocolate graham cracker, crushed
- 1/2 cup almond milk
- 1 1/2 cups ice cubes
- 1 scoop chocolate protein powder
- Pinch of salt

Directions:

1. Add all ingredients into the blender container. Secure the lid.
2. Start the blending on low speed, then quickly increase to highest speed and blend for 1 minute or until smooth.
3. Serve and enjoy.

Nutritional Value (Amount per Serving):

- Calories 399
- Fat 32 g
- Carbohydrates 18 g
- Sugar 10 g
- Protein 13 g
- Cholesterol 20 mg

Conclusion

Do you own a powerful blender like the Vitamix, and are you interested in making delicious blender dishes that can help you meet your health goals? Then this book is for you.

Throughout the Vitamix Blender Cookbook 2021, you'll find helpful tips for a nutritious blender diet. Whether you want to make a smoothie, a hearty soup, or a delicious dip, this cookbook will enhance your meals and snacks with outstanding Vitamix blender recipes everyone will love.

It's not always easy or convenient for busy people with hectic schedules to make healthy and delicious meals. Learn the secret to preparing dozens of delicious, all-natural recipes with your Vitamix blender.

CPSIA information can be obtained
at www.ICGtesting.com
Printed in the USA
LVHW111610310122
709865LV00011B/898